MATH
Motivators

by Cindy Karwowski

Illustrated by
Chris Olsen

Publisher
Instructional Fair • TS Denison
Grand Rapids, Michigan

Math Motivators

About the Book

Wake up sluggish students and start your morning or math sessions with a bang! *Math Motivators* features a wide variety of math situations addressing basic math concepts along with higher order thinking. Have fun with your students as they solve these humorously illustrated math problems.

The Answer Key is at the end of the book.

About the Author

Cindy Karwowski, a primary teacher with 25 years of experience, has written several books for Instructional Fair. She holds a bachelor's degree from Carthage College in Kenosha, Wisconsin, and a master's degree from Michigan State University.

Cindy has served on numerous curriculum committees, received an Excellence in Teaching Award, and was twice a finalist for Michigan Teacher of the Year.

Credits

Author: Cindy Karwowski
Cover Artist: Cindy Cutler
Illustrator: Chris Olsen
Project Director/Editor: Alyson Kieda
Editors: Sue Sutton, Sharon Kirkwood
Production: Pat Geasler

Standard Book Number: 1-56822-276-9
Math Motivators
Copyright © 1996 by Instructional Fair • TS Denison
2400 Turner Avenue NW
Grand Rapids, MI 49544
All Rights Reserved • Printed in the USA

Draw each silly fish by following the directions.

1. Draw a zebra fish with half as many stripes as there are inches on a ruler.

2. Draw a lionfish with a crown that has $8 + 6 - 7$ points.

3. Draw a leopard fish with this many spots: one ten + two ones.

Unscramble each boxed number word and draw the picture.

1. a tiny mouse with **xis** hats

2. a kitty with **veeeln** whiskers

3. an alligator with **ywnett-wto** teeth

4. a puppy with **gieht** bones

Write each pair of addends that could equal the number in the center of each phone.

Write the correct sign for each problem.

a. fifteen
$\bigcirc$ eight
_____
seven

b. nine
$\bigcirc$ three
_____
twelve

c. seventeen
$\bigcirc$ eight
_____
nine

d. five
$\bigcirc$ five
_____
zero

e. six
$\bigcirc$ five
_____
eleven

IF8359 Math Motivato

Cathy Cutup has a Betty the Beauty Doll. Betty's hair is 48 inches long. How many times can Cathy cut off ½ foot of Betty's hair until she becomes "Betty Buzz Cut"?

7

Tim's Terrific Time Machine has a few loose screws. It will only take him 5 minutes to tighten them. Write the time 5 minutes **before** and 5 minutes **after** each time given.

___ 8:15 ___   ___ 5:00 ___

___ 2:45 ___   ___ 6:55 ___

___ 3:05 ___   ___ 11:30 ___

 IF8359 Math Motivato

Use a calculator. How many gumballs of each color are there?

red $= (6 \times 6 + 24 \div 2 + 8)$

green $= (25 + 61 - 6 \div 4)$

blue $= (99 \div 3 + 7 - 15)$

yellow $= (50 - 18 \div 8 \times 6)$

purple $= (21 \times 2 + 8 \div 2)$

pink $= (37 + 15 \times 2 - 74)$

What's the number?

1. The tens digit is 6 less than 9. The ones digit is 4 greater than 1.

   The number is . . .

2. The ones digit is < 2 and > 0. The tens digit is 3 less than 6.

   The number is . . .

IF8359 Math Motivat

POGS! POGS! POGS!

How many POGS does each cow have?

Elsie has 56.

Daisy has twice as many as Elsie.

Bessie has half as many as Elsie.

Flossie has three times as many as Bessie.

Which is more? How much more?

a. 3 boxes of 5 golf balls
OR
2 boxes of 10 golf balls

b. 5 sacks of 10 jacks
OR
6 sacks of 8 jacks

c. 3 bags of 6 marbles
OR
4 bags of 5 marbles

How long is each slide at Neptune's Waterland?

1. The length of slide #1 is an even number between 56 and 59.

2. The length of slide #2 equals 8 x 9 + 36.

3. The length of slide #3 equals the length of slide #2 – 15.

There are 24 ghosts in Casper's haunted house who want to form haunting teams.

1. How many 2-person teams can they make?

2. How many 3-person teams can they make?

3. How many 4-person teams can they make?

4. How many 6-person teams can they make?

Help Presto the Magician put the correct number of bunnies in each hat.

a. $4 +$  $= 7$

b. $12 - 4 =$

c. $+ 8 = 15$

d. $18 - = 9$

Write the sign (+ or –) in each circle to make each problem correct.

a. 15 ◯ 8 ◯ 4 = 11

b. 5 ◯ 9 ◯ 7 = 7

c. 18 ◯ 9 ◯ 6 = 15

d. 4 ◯ 6 ◯ 4 = 6

IF8359 Math Motivat

FERGUS FISHERS FISHING FESTIVAL

Who won first place, second place, and third place?

Contestant	Weight of Fish
Goldie	2 lbs. 2 oz.
Toona	30 oz.
Starr	36 oz.

Find each player's final score at Minnie's Mini-Golf.

Eddie	Nettie	Freddy	Betty
4	2	3	1
2	3	4	5
1	5	2	3
3	1	2	2
+2	+4	+3	+2

Find the total cost of each order.

Bubba's Burger Castle

Hamburger .... 50¢
Cheeseburger .... 60¢
Chicken Chunks .... 75¢
French Fries .... 50¢, 75¢, $1.00
Onion Rings .... 75¢
Soft Drinks .... 50¢, 60¢, 70¢

a. 1 cheeseburger
    1 medium fries
    1 large soft drink

b. 1 order of chicken chunks
    1 order of onion rings
    1 medium soft drink

c. 2 hamburgers
    1 large fries
    1 small soft drink

Crawford Crocodile brushed five of his teeth at a time for one minute. If it took him 15 minutes to brush all of his teeth, how many teeth does he have?

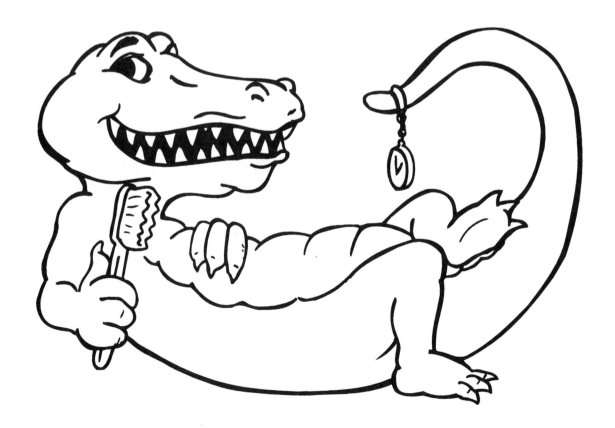

IF8359 Math Motivat

1. Which 2 areas on the target would give you a total score of 8?

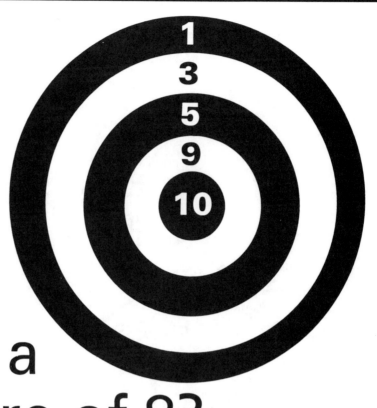

2. How many times would you have to hit the bull's-eye to get a score of 100?

3. Which 3 areas on the target would give you a total score of 20?

Michael tossed 30 pieces of clothing into the laundry. Only 7 socks, 2 shirts, and 5 shorts made it into the basket. How many pieces missed the basket?

IF8359 Math Motivat

Swim Team Laps

Minnows.. 2 laps	Sharks...... 7 laps
Dolphins .. 4 laps	Whales.... 10 laps

1. How many more laps did the Sharks swim than the Minnows?

2. How many more laps did the Whales swim than the Dolphins?

3. How many total laps did the four teams swim?

Star Theater

Sky Mountain.... 12:00 P.M.–12:52 P.M.

Power Man .... 12:10 P.M.– 1:25 P.M.

Adventures of Mortimer

    Mouse .... 12:45 P.M.– 1:55 P.M.

Hidden Treasure.... 1:35 P.M.– 3:05 P.M

Turtle Pond......... 12:45 P.M.– 1:55 P.M.

The Grogs .... 2:15 P.M.– 3:00 P.M.

★ ★ ★ ★ ★ ★ ★ ★ ★ ★ ★ ★ ★ ★

How long is each movie?

IF8359 Math Motivat

1. What does Freddie do most?

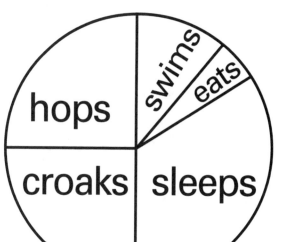

2. What does Freddie do least?

3. Does Freddie hop or swim more often?

4. What takes Freddie about the same amount of time as croaking?

The Queen of Hearts was baking cookies. Each tray took 25 minutes to bake.

Complete the chart.

Tray	Put in Oven	Took out of Oven
1	10:30 A.M.	
2	11:00 A.M.	
3	12:10 P.M.	
4	12:50 P.M.	

Use your calculator to find out who said . . .

MY POP'S SWEETER THAN YOUR POP!

Enter: one hundred

x	100
+	7,777
−	seventy

= Flip calculator over!

Racer	Number of Laps
Flash	5
Lightning	8
Speedy	11

If the track is ½ mile long, how far did each racer travel?

Complete each set of dog tags by writing the number that comes before and the number that comes after the given number.

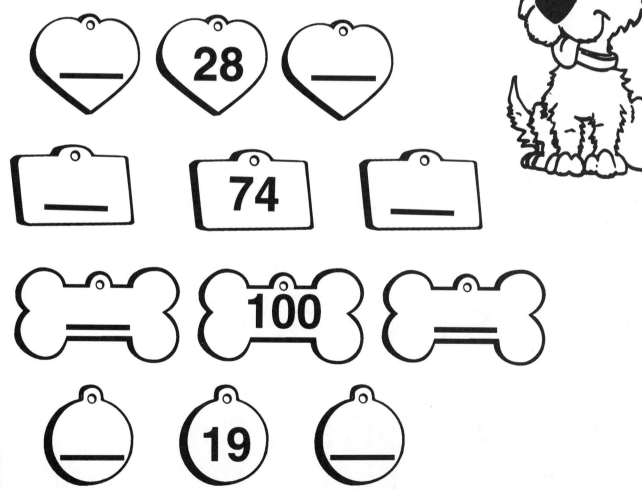

The results of the big race are in! Dasher crossed the finish line at 1:15 P.M., Dancer finished 15 minutes later, and Rudolph completed the race ½ hour before Dasher.

a. At what times did Dancer and Rudolph cross the line?

b. Who won?

How many legs does each set of animals have?

a. 3 horses

b. 4 cows

c. 8 ducks

d. 7 sheep

e. 10 chicks

f. 5 pigs

g. 6 goats

h. 9 geese

Write 2 addition and 2 subtraction problems about the Penguin family.

Write 2 addition and 2 subtraction problems on the Polar Bear family.

For every lie Pinocchio told, his nose grew 3 inches.

Day	Number of Lies
Sunday	1
Monday	2
Tuesday	5
Wednes.	4
Thurs.	2
Friday	1
Saturday	1

1. How many inches did his nose grow in one week?

2. How many feet?

What is the number on each honey pot?

a. 4 hundreds
+
9 tens
+
0 ones

b. 5 tens
+
1 hundred
+
8 ones

c. 2 ones
+
6 tens
+
4 hundreds

d. 3 hundreds
+
5 ones
+
7 tens

IF8359 Math Motivat

Write the number each robot would compute if you fed it the number 6.

What if you fed each robot the number 8?

Pokey, Molasses, Tardy, and Slowly had a race. Although Pokey didn't win, he wasn't last. Molasses finished directly ahead of Pokey. Tardy finished right behind Slowly.

RACER 286

RACE 543

RAC 74

RACE 482

Write the names in the order they finished the race.

Morticia's Peculiar Pets

37¢

55¢

70¢

96¢

You buy 2 boa constrictors, 3 tarantulas, 1 vampire bat, and 4 octopi.

How much is your bill?

Poor Mama Monster's children are sick. Their normal temperature is 83°F. What is each one's temperature now?

1. Hairy's temperature rose 63°.

2. Whisker's temperature dropped 51°.

3. Stubble's temperature went up 49°.

4. Topknot's temperature went down 38°.

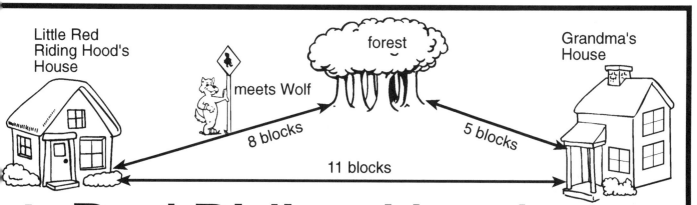

Little Red Riding Hood's House

meets Wolf

forest

Grandma's House

8 blocks

5 blocks

11 blocks

1. Red Riding Hood met Wolf halfway to the forest. How far had she gone? She went on to Grandma's house. How far did she travel altogether?

2. How much shorter was the path that led directly from Red's house to Grandma's?

Find the larger number in each pair and write its letter to answer the riddle . . .

What did the frog like best about France?

56 65	83 79	75 48	96 99	145 99	88 180
B F	R A	E L	R N	C S	I H

74 69	76 19	56 67	97 79	619 69
F C	L A	O I	E G	S D

IF8359 Math Motivato

Freddy Freckleface had 162 freckles. He asked the genie to remove 156. The genie said he could remove no more than 50 freckles per wish.

1. If Freddy had three wishes, how many total freckles could the genie remove?

2. How many freckles would Freddy have left?

Help Yodel A. Eeo climb up and down the mountains. When he climbs up a mountain, add the numbers. When he comes down, subtract. What is the final number?

Start with 6.

1 4 6 6 4 3 5 8 7 9

End

1. Which sets of two numbers have a sum of 11?

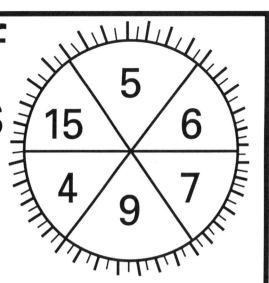

2. Which two numbers have a difference of 6?

3. Which sets of two numbers have a sum of 13?

4. Which two numbers have a difference of 8?

5. Which three numbers have a sum of 15?

Chef Mac A. Roni had only one 50-ft. piece of spaghetti in his pot. He needed to divide it equally among 5 customers.

1. How many feet would each person receive?

2. If the chef then cut each person's amount into 6" pieces, how many pieces would each get?

Penny counted her money. She had 2 nickels, a quarter, 9 pennies, and 5 dimes.

1. How much money had Penny saved?

2. How much more did she need to equal one dollar?

Which statements about the following numbers are true?

1 2 3 4 5 6 7 8 9

1. There are more odd than even numbers shown.

2. The last four numbers equal more than the first five numbers.

3. The largest 2-digit number you can make is 89.

Timmy and Tommy, twin brothers, invented a machine that can double anything.

Double each item.

6 blocks   15 drums

9 kites   22 toy cars

The teeny-tiny woman loves to count tiny things. Help her total each problem.

a.
$$45 + 98$$

b.
$$156 + 372$$

c.
$$89 + 53$$

d.
$$16 + 64$$

e.
$$483 + 118$$

f.
$$786 + 165$$

Page, the bookworm, needs to straighten four shelves of library books. Help her arrange them from the least to the greatest.

154   164   159   144   160

176   184   189   155   178

254   245   215   209   251

399   378   345   344   361

My front tooth fell out, so I put it under my pillow. In the morning I found 15¢ in place of my tooth. How many different sets of coins could I have?

IF8359 Math Motivato

Scruffy McGrew collects baseball cards. He keeps 9 cards in each box. So far he has 5 boxes.

1. How many cards does he have altogether?

2. How many cards will he have altogether if he fills 3 more boxes?

Uh oh! Some clocks need new batteries. Which ones don't show the correct time?

a. 8:10

b. 1:45

c. 9:30

d. 1:30

e. 5:55

Show what comes next.

1. 2, 4, 6, 8, 10, 12, _____

2. 45, 40, 35, 30, 25, _____

3. 86, 88, 90, 92, 94, _____

4. ⊙, ⊙⊙, ▣, ▣▣, ▽, _____

5. A, B, C, D, E, F, G, _____

6. H, K, N, Q, T, W, _____

7. ¢, ¢, $, ¢, ¢, _____

8. ▽, □, ○, ▽, □, _____

Draw a monster by giving it . . .

- a square head.

- 4 circle eyes.

- 2 oval ears.

- 6 triangular teeth.

- a hexagon body.

- rectangular arms and legs.

Name your monster.

Copy the problems.
Circle the two numbers
in each that equal **ten**.
Then work each
problem.

```
   7          4          5
   2          6          3
 + 8        + 2        + 7
 ___        ___        ___
```

```
   1          8
   5          5
 + 9        + 5
 ___        ___
```

Help Mindy solve each problem.

a. an even number greater than 6 and less than 10

b. 6 plus 6 minus 5

c. an odd number less than 9 and greater than 5

d. $4 + 6 + 5 - 9$

e. $24 - 6 + 3 - 7 + 5$

A little mermaid, an octopus, and a lobster were swimming in a line. The one with claws swam in the middle. The one with a fish tail swam in back.

In what order were the three friends swimming?

Help Ed decide which vegetables he planted in each of 10 rows.

- Corn is planted in the last 3 rows.

- The first 3 rows contain carrots.

- Two rows of beans are in front of the corn.

- Between the carrots and beans lie 2 rows of peas.

Rufus Goofus told his mother he could write the correct sum for each addition problem in one minute. Can you?

$$5 \quad\quad 7 \quad\quad 8 \quad\quad 9 \quad\quad 3$$
$$+8 \quad\quad +2 \quad\quad +4 \quad\quad +5 \quad\quad +7$$

$$4 \quad\quad 6 \quad\quad 5 \quad\quad 2 \quad\quad 1$$
$$+5 \quad\quad +6 \quad\quad +3 \quad\quad +9 \quad\quad +8$$

Follow the path and add or subtract each number to discover what number waits at the finish line.

8 +7 -2 -3 +6 -8 +4 +5 -9 +0

On Monday, Lucky Leprechaun had 122 pieces of gold. On Tuesday, he lost five pieces. On Wednesday, he found ten more. How many pieces does he have altogether?

Write the numerals for each number word.

a. thirteen

b. twenty-four

c. forty-six

d. ninety-eight

e. one hundred seven

f. one hundred fifty-one

g. five hundred twelve

h. two hundred sixty-two

The absent-minded scientist counts backwards and sometimes forgets numbers. What numbers did he forget?

a. 12, 11, 10, ___, ___, 7, ___

b. 39, ___, ___, 36, ___, ___

c. 175, ___, ___, ___, 171, ___

d. 207, 206, ___, 204, ___, ___

e. 761, ___, ___, 758, ___, ___

Lee's Iced Tea

Iced Tea .... 25¢
1 Lemon Slice .... 10¢
Sugar .... 5¢

Each member of the track team decided to buy a glass of iced tea "with the works."

1. How much did each runner pay?

2. How much was the total for all six runners?

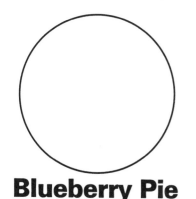 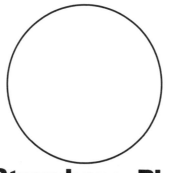 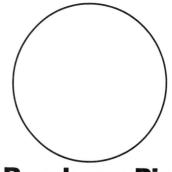

Blueberry Pie   **Strawberry Pie**   **Raspberry Pie**

1. Divide the strawberry pie into fourths. Show that ¾ of the pie was eaten.

2. Divide the raspberry pie into sixths. Show that ⅘ was eaten.

3. Divide the blueberry pie into eighths. Show that ⅝ was eaten.

Work each problem.
Write the letters of the
corresponding answers
to solve the riddle.

$$\begin{array}{r} 56 \\ -\ 27 \\ \hline \text{(i)} \end{array} \qquad \begin{array}{r} 90 \\ -\ 83 \\ \hline \text{(h)} \end{array} \qquad \begin{array}{r} 135 \\ -108 \\ \hline \text{(r)} \end{array}$$

$$\begin{array}{r} 268 \\ -129 \\ \hline \text{(c)} \end{array} \qquad \begin{array}{r} 567 \\ -196 \\ \hline \text{(a)} \end{array}$$

What has arms and legs but no head?

139	7	371	29	27

Help Lookout B. Low find the missing numbers so he can find how many feet below sea level his sub should be.

$$
\begin{array}{r}
5\;6\;\square \\
-\;1\;\square\;2 \\
\hline
\square\;2\;1
\end{array}
\qquad
\begin{array}{r}
\square\;5\;9 \\
-\;5\;2\;\square \\
\hline
3\;\square\;6
\end{array}
\qquad
\begin{array}{r}
4\;\square\;0 \\
-\;\square\;1\;0 \\
\hline
2\;1\;\square
\end{array}
$$

$$
\begin{array}{r}
7\;8\;\square \\
-\;\square\;3\;4 \\
\hline
3\;\square\;1
\end{array}
\qquad
\begin{array}{r}
\square\;4\;6 \\
-\;7\;\square\;3 \\
\hline
2\;1\;\square
\end{array}
$$

Write each row of numbers in order from least to greatest.

a. 29, 17, 12, 22, 20

b. 56, 47, 33, 29, 74

c. 101, 110, 115, 106, 114

d. 332, 451, 297, 279, 199

e. 602, 598, 620, 589, 600

IF8359 Math Motivato

Cinderella's stepsisters bought jewelry from Sleazy Slick to wear at the ball.

The first stepsister chose a glass ring for 45¢ and a fake pearl necklace for 75¢.

The second stepsister bought a tinfoil crown for 90¢ and a plastic bracelet for 25¢.

1. Which "big spender" spent more?

2. How much more did she spend?

The first kitten lost his mitten on Friday.

The second kitten lost his mitten 4 days later.

The third kitten lost her mitten two days after the second lost his.

On which days of the week did the second and third kittens lose their mittens?

Mortimer Mouse
is 4 inches tall.

Maxine Mouse
is 2 inches taller
than Mortimer.

Kirby Cat is 2 feet tall.

1. How many Mortimers
   would it take to equal
   the height of Kirby?

2. How many Maxines
   would it take to equal
   the height of Kirby?

Mulligan Muscleman liked to lift weights.

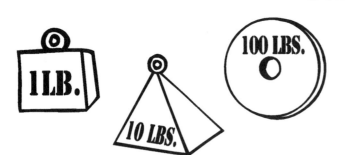

Use the weight codes to find out how many pounds he lifted on each try.

a.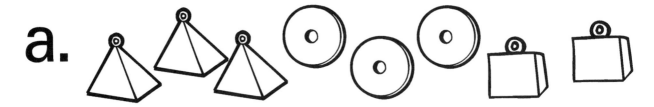

b.

Millie Model has three
blouses and four skirts.

How many different
outfits can she model?

Marvo Mathematics knows the missing numbers. Do you?

a.
$$3\square5$$
$$+\ \square64$$
$$\overline{48\square}$$

b.
$$\square79$$
$$+\ 6\square0$$
$$\overline{97\square}$$

c.
$$65\square$$
$$+\ 2\square8$$
$$\overline{\square99}$$

d.
$$4\square1$$
$$+\ \square53$$
$$\overline{86\square}$$

e.
$$\square72$$
$$+\ 61\square$$
$$\overline{9\square5}$$

IF8359 Math Motivat

When the cow jumped over the moon, she counted 75 craters in all. If one-half of the moon had 34 craters, how many were on the other half?

Work each problem to solve the riddle.

$$\begin{array}{r} 16 \\ +12 \\ \hline \end{array}$$
(u)

$$\begin{array}{r} 8 \\ +3 \\ \hline \end{array}$$
(h)

$$\begin{array}{r} 25 \\ -13 \\ \hline \end{array}$$
(a)

$$\begin{array}{r} 10 \\ -5 \\ \hline \end{array}$$
(s)

$$\begin{array}{r} 31 \\ +44 \\ \hline \end{array}$$
(q)

What was the little monster's favorite vegetable?

5	75	28	12	5	11

IF8359 Math Motivate

Millie rode the Tilt-a-Whirl 8 + 7 times.

Tillie rode the Tilt-a-Whirl 9 + 3 times.

Willie rode the Tilt-a-Whirl 9 + 9 times.

Billy rode the Tilt-a-Whirl 6 + 8 times.

a. Who rode the Tilt-a-Whirl the most?

b. Who rode it the least?

Humpty Dumpty built a new wall. The first three rows looked like this.

If the finished wall was eight rows high, how many bricks would Humpty need?

 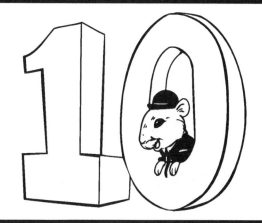

| 67 | 56 | 7 | 90 | 21 | 48 |
| 33 | 71 | 5 | 82 | 27 | |

Which numbers are . . .

a. between 55 and 99?

b. larger than 68?

c. smaller than 34?

d. even?

e. odd?

Use your calculator to find the location of the doctor's office.

Enter: seven

- $\boxed{\times}$ two
- $\boxed{+}$ 95
- $\boxed{-}$ nine
- $\boxed{\div}$ five

$=$ Flip calculator over!

Use your calculator to find the following:

a. three numbers in sequence that give the sum of 9

b. three numbers in sequence that give the sum of 15

c. the sum of the numbers 1 through 10

Use Mr. Double Bubble's special bubbles to answer:

1. Which numbers are **not** part of the circle bubble?

2. Which number is in both the circle bubble and the triangle bubble?

3. Which number is in both the square bubble and the circle bubble?

4. Which numbers are **not** in the circle bubble or the square bubble?

Jack and Jill raced to fill a tub with water. Jack carried a bucket every five minutes, and Jill carried one every six minutes. After one hour, how many buckets did each carry?

Poor Little Bo Peep! She's lost three-fourths of her flock of 32 sheep. How many does she have left?

IF8359 Math Motivato

Kay Nine has a great set of shiny, green teeth. The number of teeth she has is greater than 75 and less than 90 and the sum of its two digits is 10.

How many shiny, green teeth does Kay Nine have?

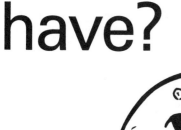

Old Mother Hubbard wants to clean her 32 cupboards. If she cleans four cupboards each hour, how long will it take?

IF8359 Math Motivato

If you give Buck, the banker, the following coins, how many 1-dollar bills can you receive in exchange for them?

Draw . . .

a. a square that is 4 squares long and 4 squares high.

b. a rectangle that is 3 squares long and 5 squares high.

c. a rectangle that is 6 squares long and half as many squares high.

Art, the artist, is studying shading. How much of each piece of fruit is shaded?

Dolly Dipit needs to fill containers with ice cream.

1. How many pints would she need to fill a quart container?

2. How many quarts would she need to fill a gallon container?

3. How many pints would she need to fill a gallon container?

Help Dorothy complete the patterns shown on the yellow brick road.

		2			0	
		4			6	
0	3		9			
1		8		18		
2		10				
3		12	16	20		
4						

Use each set of numbers to write two addition and two subtraction problems.

a. 7   15   8

b. 14   5   9

c. 5   7   12

d. 16   9   7

Which is probably the length of . . .

a. a frog?
4 cm   4 in.   4 ft.

b. a hot dog?
36 cm   36 in.   36 ft.

c. a hog?
5 yd.   5 in.   5 ft.

Captain Kirko's time machine can be set to travel in both the past and the future.

For each year, write **before** or **after** to tell if it is in the past or in the future.

a. 1776   d. 1895

b. 1492   e. 2089

c. 2000   f. 1989

Every time Mr. Jack-in-the-Box jumps up, he holds the number that comes next in a pattern.

What number would he hold up next for each pattern?

a. 15, 20, 25, 30, 35, ___

b. 27, 30, 33, 36, 39, ___

c. 1, 7, 13, 19, 25, ___

Which takes less time . . .

1. eating lunch OR brushing your teeth?

2. sharpening a pencil OR cleaning your room?

3. going down the slide OR reading a book?

4. doing 30 addition problems OR eating a candy bar?

5. playing *Monopoly* OR combing your hair?

Write the correct temperature for each picture.

a. 25°F / 52° F

b. 95°F / 59°F

c. 212°F / 21°F

d. 9°F / 90°F

COTTON CANDY 85¢

POPCORN 95¢

ICE CREAM 65¢

POP 55¢

How much change would each child get if . . .

1. Jim gave the vendor $1.00 for popcorn.

2. Cindy gave the vendor 9 dimes for cotton candy.

3. Grace gave the vendor 3 quarters for ice cream.

Complete the pattern on the last dinosaur in each family.

Red Riding Hood's basket for Grandma contained 5 apples, 16 grapes, and some bananas and oranges. How many bananas and oranges were inside if there were half as many oranges as grapes and twice as many bananas as apples?

Name of Contestant	Number of Snowmen Built
Chilly Willy	☃ ☃ ☃ ☃
Ice Bucket	☃ ☃ ⌡
Mr. Shivers	☃ ☃ ☃ ☃ ☃ ☃ ☃
Popsicle	☃ ☃ ☃
Snowflake	☃ ☃ ☃ ☃

Key: = **2 snowmen**

1. Who built the most snowmen?

2. Who built the same number of snowmen?

3. Who built 5 snowmen?

Name each shape. Then add a face to each one.

a.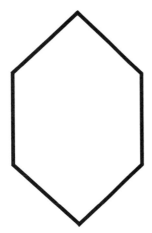

b.

c.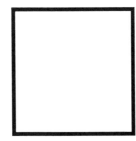

d.

e.

How many pieces of Chef Luigi's Pizza Supreme did each one eat if . . .

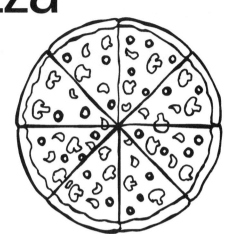

1. Dick ate ⅜ of the pizza?

2. Jane ate ¼ of the pizza?

3. Sally ate ⅛ of the pizza?

4. Spot ate the rest?

Create your own picture to represent each number sentence.

a. $4 + 2 = 6$

b. $1 + 3 = 4$

c. $5 - 3 = 2$

d. $3 - 2 = 1$

Little Dipper loves to count stars but he forgets some numbers. Help him by filling in the blanks.

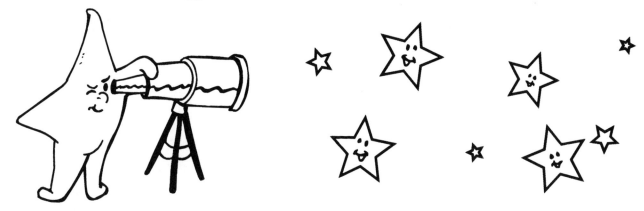

a. 1, 2, __, __, 5, __, 7, __

b. 16, __, 18, __, __, __, 22

c. 47, 48, __, __, 51, 52, __

d. 79, __, __, 82, 83, __, __

e. __, 93, __, __, __, 97, 98

Half of each group of baby animals were taken to the barn nursery. How many were left to play in the play "pen"?

IF8359 Math Motivat

Char Broil is cooking hamburgers and hot dogs. She can have five items on the grill at one time. Draw the different combinations of hot dogs and hamburgers.

1. How much does Mrs. Sprat weigh if she weighs three times as much as Jack?

2. How much does Jack Jr. weigh if he weighs half as much as Jack?

IF8359 Math Motivat·

Noah's Animal Crackers

contains 1 pair of . . .

- lions
- bears
- parrots
- tigers
- doves
- snakes

1. How many animal crackers are there altogether?

2. How many are members of the cat family?

3. How many are birds?

4. How many are reptiles?

The three Pig brothers decided to build a log house together. If each wall needed 25 logs, how many logs would they need?

IF8359 Math Motivate

Cartoon Carnival

1:00 – Moses Moose on
       the Loose

1:30 – Woody Woodchopper

2:00 – Dudley Duck Dives In

2:30 – Petula Pig Pigs-out

1. What cartoon could Telly Vision watch at 1:30?

2. What show could he watch an hour later?

3. What could he watch between Woody and Petula?

Which sentence is probably correct?

1. The baby weighs 7 lbs.
   The baby weighs 7 oz.

2. The adult elephant weighs 30 tons.
   The adult elephant weighs 1 ton.

3. The dinosaur weighs 900 g.
   The dinosaur weighs 900 kg.

Write the date of each Farkle's birthday.

1. Farrell Farkle's birthday is on Halloween.

2. Farrah Farkle's is 2 days before Farrell's birthday.

3. Farley Farkle's is 5 days after Farrah's birthday.

4. Fario Farkle's is the day after Farrell's birthday.

Name each shape Selina Seal balances on her nose.

IF8359 Math Motivato

Use the numbers in the soup to help Coretta Cook write . . .

a. the least and greatest 2-digit numbers.

b. the least and greatest 3-digit numbers.

c. the least and greatest 4-digit numbers.

Maui Monkey drank 3 quarts of coconut juice. Maya Monkey drank one gallon.

1. Who drank more coconut juice?

2. How much more did she drink?

IF8359 Math Motivato

Simple Simon met a pie man who balanced 24 pies on his right hand and 28 pies on his left.

1. How many pies did he balance altogether?

2. How many more pies did he balance on his left hand?

Draw holes in the rest of Mortimer Mouse's cheese following the pattern.

1

2

3

4

5

IF8359 Math Motivato

Help Tidy Tillie arrange the cans on each shelf from the least to the greatest by numbering each can in order.

a.

 45 oz.  16 oz.  22 oz.  60 oz.  36 oz.

b.

 9 oz.  21 oz.  3 oz.  12 oz.  30 oz.

The first beanstalk is 3 feet taller than the third. The second is 2 feet shorter than the first. The third is 83 feet tall. How tall are the other two beanstalks?

IF8359 Math Motiva

Help the royal locksmith find the correct key to open Queen Goldie's locks.

1. 🔒 $+ 9 = 11$

2. $7 +$ 🔒 $= 15$

3. 🔒 $+ 8 = 17$

4. $15 -$ 🔒 $= 9$

5. $18 - 9 =$ 🔒

6. $14 -$ 🔒 $= 6$

King Kareem ordered his knights to guard the palace's 48 windows. If there were two knights posted at each window, how many knights were on duty?

IF8359 Math Motivat

Add the numbers in each set the juggler juggled.

a. 3 tens   6 hundreds   5 ones

b. 4 hundreds   7 ones   8 tens

c. 3 hundreds   8 tens   5 ones

d. 1 hundred   5 ones   0 tens

Become a super math detective and discover the numbers represented by each shape.

a. $\heartsuit + \heartsuit = 14$

b. $\heartsuit + \square = 9$

c. $16 - \bigcirc = \bigcirc$

d. $\bigcirc - \square = 6$

Miss Muffet was totally disgusted! Seven spiders sat right down beside her. How many ugly, little legs did she see?

Write the number word that rhymes with each picture.

A.
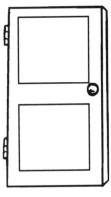

E.

F.

B.

G.

H.

C.

I.

D.

J.

Arthur Artist loved to draw shapes, shapes, and more shapes!

Count the number of shapes in each picture.

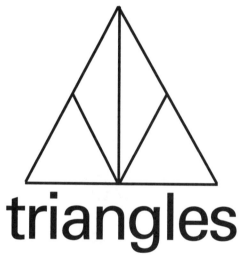

triangles

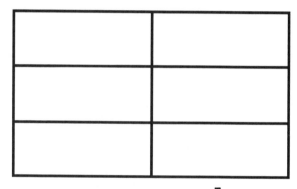

rectangles

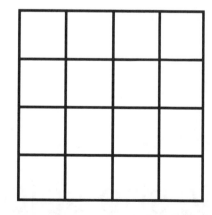

squares

Copy and complete the graph using the following information.

	0	2	4	6	8	10
Monday						
Tuesday						
Wednesday						
Thursday						
Friday						

1. On Monday, Polly Pucker sold 8 cups of lemonade.

2. On Tuesday, she sold 2 cups more than on Wednesday.

3. On Wednesday, she sold 2 cups less than on Monday.

4. On Thursday, she sold 1 cup more than on Monday.

5. On Friday, she sold 1 cup less than on Thursday.

Use a calculator to pull each answer from the hat.

a. 56 x 21 + 26 − 83 =

b. 99 ÷ 9 x 11 + 89 =

c. 168 − 32 + 71 x 40 =

d. 100 − 25 ÷ 5 x 46 =

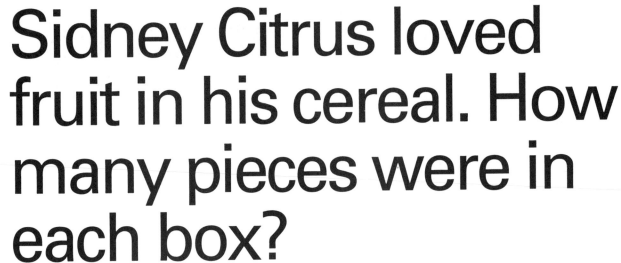

Sidney Citrus loved fruit in his cereal. How many pieces were in each box?

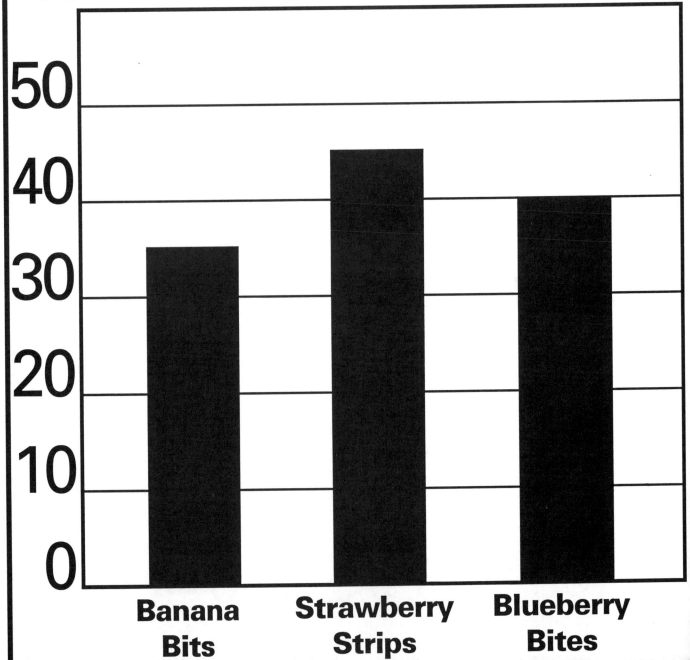

Drucilla Dragon lit marshmallows at the campground.

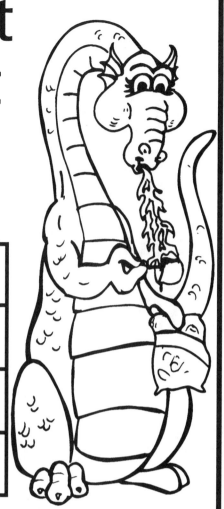

Week	Marshmallows
1	21
2	23
3	25
4	27

1. How many marsh-mallows did she light the first four weeks?

2. How many would she probably light on week 5?

Standing in the window of the tall tower, Rapunzel gently loosed her golden hair. If her hair were 1 foot longer than the 600-inch tower, how many feet long would her hair be?

IF8359 Math Motivato

Mr. Rabbit was late again! The tea party began at 2:15 P.M. He arrived 25 minutes late. What time did he arrive?

The golden goose had a busy day! She laid an egg every 5 minutes.

1. How many eggs did she lay in one hour?

2. How many dozen eggs did she lay in that 24-hour period?

Poor Frosty! The sun was shining brightly, and he was beginning to melt. Each hour he shrank two inches. If he were originally 60 inches tall, how tall would he be in 4 hours?

If Evelyn Evans prefers even numbers, which of the following would she choose?

48   15   765

67   552   83

25   536

54

33

89   911

852

Gepetto was busy attaching hands to the clocks to show the correct times. Add the hands to help him.

5:45

1:30

8:10

6:25

Gordie Gorilla eats bananas by the bunch. The first bunch had six bananas. The second bunch had four more bananas than the first. The third bunch had three bananas less than the second. How many bananas did Gordie eat altogether?

Mr. Easter Bunny has five eggs in his basket. If the eggs are pink, yellow, and lavender, how many of each color could there be? Find all of the combinations.

Lately, Mr. Groundhog has seen his shadow only on odd-numbered years. If this continues to happen, how many times will he see it between 1996 and 2010?

Poor Old Woman in the Shoe had too many windows to do. If she has the same number of windows on the back of her house, how many windows does she have to clean altogether?

Santa's elves placed the presents in three piles. The first pile had six presents. How many presents were in the other two piles if the second pile had twice as many presents as the first, and the third pile had five more presents than the second?

Tom Turkey collects drumsticks. If he has fifteen pairs, how many drumsticks does he own?

Puddles Puppy buries three bones in each hole she digs. If she dug six holes, how many bones did she bury?

IF8359 Math Motivato

Kirby Kitty is nine months older than Kelsey Kitty and three months younger than Katy Kitty. If Kelsey was born in March, in what months were Kirby and Katy born?

The Seven Dwarfs found some amazing diamonds. They were ½ blue and ½ white. Copy each diamond and color ½ of it blue.

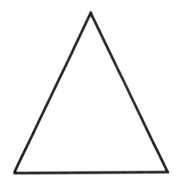

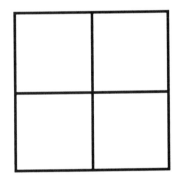

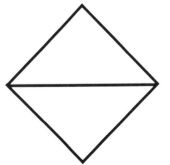
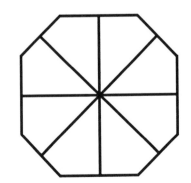

146

At midnight, Cinderella's beautiful dress turned into rags. What time did the coach turn back into a pumpkin if it happened 15 minutes later?

Mary, Mary Quite Contrary planted her lovely flowers in the following pattern.

Draw and color the next three flowers.

Four perky penguins stood in a line. Patty was first, and Paul was third. Where were Priscilla and Petula if Priscilla stood between Paul and Patty?

Which piggy has the most money?

4 dimes
1 quarter
3 pennies

Porky

Patty

3 nickels
1 dime
2 quarters

6 pennies
3 dimes
2 quarters

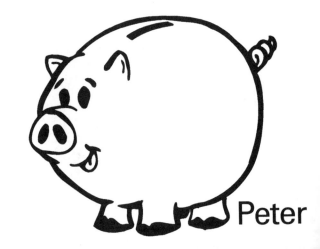

Peter

IF8359 Math Motivate

Maynard Mailman sold five stamps. How much did they cost altogether?

32¢

33¢

18¢

27¢

29¢

The candle of the first jack-o'-lantern went out at 10:30 P.M. The candle of the second went out 15 minutes later. The candle of the third went out one hour after the first. When did the second and third jack-o'-lanterns go out?

Cecilia Centipede buys her gym shoes by the dozen. If she buys seven dozen pairs of shoes so that each foot can have a new shoe, how many feet does she have?

After Monstro swallowed Pinocchio, there was little for Pinocchio to do but count fish. He counted 25 fish, then 39 fish, and then 47 more. How many fish did he count altogether?

Papa, Mama, and Baby Bear each ate a different breakfast. Papa's meal contained meat and Mama added milk to hers. Who ate each breakfast?

If a bag of 20 peanuts costs 25¢, and a bag of 45 peanuts costs 50¢, which is a better deal for Elmer Elephant?

IF8359 Math Motivat

Lionel Lion roared every ½ hour. If he began roaring at 6:00 A.M., at what time did he roar the tenth time?

Answer Key

Page 3
1. zebra fish—6 stripes
2. lionfish—7 points
3. leopard fish—12 spots

Page 4
1. six
2. eleven
3. twenty-two
4. eight

Page 5

$$\frac{3}{2+1} \qquad \frac{6}{5+1} \qquad \frac{7}{6+1} \qquad \frac{10}{9+1}$$

$$4+2 \qquad 5+2 \qquad 8+2$$
$$4+3 \qquad 7+3$$
$$6+4$$

Page 6
a. –   b. +   c. –   d. –   e. +

Page 7
8 times

Page 8

8:10	8:15	8:20	4:55	5:00	5:05
2:40	2:45	2:50	6:50	6:55	7:00
3:00	3:05	3:10	11:25	11:30	11:35

Page 9
red—38   blue—25   purple—25
green—20   yellow—24   pink—30

Page 10
1. 35   2. 31

Page 11
Daisy—112   Bessie—28   Flossie—84

Page 12
a. 2 boxes of 10 golf balls; 5 more
b. 5 sacks of 10 jacks; 2 more
c. 4 bags of 5 marbles; 2 more

Page 13
Slide 1—58   Slide 2—108   Slide 3—93

Page 14
1. 12   2. 8   3. 6   4. 4

Page 15
a. 3   b. 8   c. 7   d. 9

Page 16
a. 15 – 8 + 4 = 11   c. 18 – 9 + 6 = 15
b. 5 + 9 – 7 = 7   d. 4 + 6 – 4 = 6

Page 17
1st—Starr   2nd—Goldie   3rd—Toona

Page 18
Eddie—12   Freddy—14   **Nettie won!**
Nettie—15   Betty—13

Page 19
A. $2.05   B. $2.10   C. $2.50

Page 20
75 teeth

Page 21
1. 5 and 3   2. 10 times   3. 10, 9, and 1

Page 22
16 items

Page 23
1. 5 laps   2. 6 laps   3. 23 laps

Page 24
Sky Mountain—52 minutes
Power Man—1 hr. 15 min.
Adventures of Mortimer Mouse—1 hr. 10 min.
Hidden Treasure—1 ½ hours
Turtle Pond—1 hr. 10 min
The Grogs—45 minutes

Page 25
1. sleeps   2. eats   3. hop   4. hopping

Page 26
Tray 1—10:55   Tray 3—12:35
Tray 2—11:25   Tray 4—1:15

Page 27
Lolli

Page 28
Flash—2 ½ miles   Speedy—5 ½ miles
Lightning—4 miles

Page 29

| 27 | 28 | 29 | 99 | 100 | 101 |
| 73 | 74 | 75 | 18 | 19 | 20 |

Page 30
Dancer—1:30   Rudolph—12:45
Rudolph won!

Page 31
3 horses = 12 legs   10 chickens = 20 legs
4 cows = 16 legs   5 pigs = 20 legs
8 ducks = 16 legs   6 goats = 24 legs
7 sheep = 28 legs   9 geese = 18 legs

Page 32

Penguins				Bears			
3	2	5	5	3	1	4	4
+ 2	+ 3	– 3	– 2	+ 1	+ 3	– 3	– 1
5	5	2	3	4	4	1	3

Page 33
1. 48 inches   2. 4 feet

Page 34
a. 490   b. 158   c. 462   d. 375

Page 35

6	8
+ 2 =8	+ 2 =10
– 2 =4	– 2 = 6
x 2 =12	x 2 =16
÷ 2 =3	÷ 2 =4

Page 36
Molasses   Pokey   Slowly   Tardy

Page 37
$6.15

Page 38
Hairy—146°   Stubble—132°
Whisker—32°   Topknot—45°

Page 39
1. 4 blocks—13 blocks altogether
2. 2 blocks

Page 40
French flies

Page 41
1. 150 freckles   2. 12

Page 42
5

Page 43
1. 7 and 4, 5 and 6   4. 15 and 7
2. 15 and 9   5. 6, 4, and 5
3. 6 and 7, 9 and 4

Page 44
1. 10 feet   2. 20 pieces

Page 45
1. 94¢   2. 6¢

Page 46
#1 and #2 are true; #3 is false

Page 47
12 blocks   30 drums
18 kites   44 toy cars

Page 48
a. 143   c. 142   e. 601
b. 528   d. 80   f. 951

Page 49
a. 144, 154, 159, 160, 164
b. 155, 176, 178, 184, 189
d. 209, 215, 245, 251, 254
d. 344, 345, 361, 378, 399

Page 50   6 different sets
1. 3 nickels   4. 1 dime and 5 pennies
2. 15 pennies   5. 1 nickel and 10 penni
3. 1 dime and 1 nickel   6. 2 nickels and 5 penni

Page 51
1. 45 cards   2. 72 cards

Page 52
a and **e** are not correct.

Page 53
1. 14   3. 96   5. H   7. $
2. 20   4. ▽   6. Z   8. ◯

Page 54   *Pictures may vary.*

Page 55

7	4	5	1	
2	6	3	5	
+ 8	+ 2	+ 7	+ 9	
17	12	15	15	1

Page 56

a. 8 b. 7 c. 7 d. 6 e. 19

Page 57

1st—octopus 3rd—mermaid
2nd—lobster

Page 58

1. carrots 4. peas 6. beans 8. corn
2 carrots 5. peas 7. beans 9. corn
3. carrots 10. corn

Page 59

5	7	8	9	3
+8	+2	+4	+5	+7
13	**9**	**12**	**14**	**10**
4	6	5	2	1
+5	+6	+3	+9	+8
9	**12**	**8**	**11**	**9**

Page 60 8

Page 61 127

Page 62

a. 13 c. 46 e. 107 g. 512
b. 24 d. 98 f. 151 h. 262

age 63

a. 9, 8, 6
b. 38, 37, 35, 34
c. 174, 173, 172, 170
d. 205, 203, 202
e. 760, 759, 757, 756

Page 64

1. 40¢ 2. $2.40

Page 65

Blueberry Strawberry Raspberry
Pie Pie Pie

age 66 chair

age 67

563	859	420	785	946
−142	−523	−210	−434	−733
421	**336**	**210**	**351**	**213**

age 68

. 12, 17, 20, 22, 29 d. 199, 279, 297, 332, 451
. 29, 33, 47, 56, 74 e. 602, 598, 620, 589, 600
. 101, 106, 110, 114, 115

age 69

1. first stepsister 2. 5¢ more

age 70 second kitten—Tuesday
third kitten—Thursday

age 71

1. 6 Mortimers 2. 4 Maxines

ge 72

a. 332 lbs. b. 322 lbs.

ge 73 12

ge 74 a. 325 b. 379 c. 651 d. 411 e. 372
+164 +600 +248 +453 +613
489 979 899 864 985

ge 75 41 craters

Page 76 squash

Page 77 a. Willie b. Tillie

Page 78 64 bricks

Page 79

a. 67, 71, 56, 82, 90 d. 56, 82, 90, 48
b. 71, 82, 90 e. 33, 67, 71, 5, 7, 27, 21
c. 33, 5, 7, 27, 21

Page 80 Oz

Page 81

a. 2, 3, 4 b. 4, 5, 6 c. 55

Page 82

1. 1, 2, 7, 8, 9 3. 6
2. 3 4. 1, 2

Page 83

Jack carried 12 buckets.
Jill carried 10 buckets.

Page 84 8 sheep

Page 85 82 teeth

Page 86 8 hours

Page 87 2 one-dollar bills

Page 88

a. b. c.

Page 89

orange—¼ apple—½ pear—½
grapes—⅜ banana—¾

Page 90

1. 2 pints 2. 4 quarts 3. 8 pints

Page 91

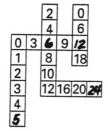

Page 92

a. 7	8	15	15
+8	+7	−7	−8
15	15	8	7
b. 5	9	14	14
+9	+5	−5	−9
14	14	9	5
c. 7	5	12	12
+5	+7	−7	−5
12	12	5	7
d. 7	9	16	16
+9	+7	−7	−9
16	16	9	7

Page 93

a. 4 in. b. 36 cm c. 5 ft.

Page 94

a. before c. after e. after
b. before d. before f. before

Page 95

a. 40 b. 42 c. 31

Page 96

1. brushing your teeth 4. eating a candy bar
2. sharpening a pencil 5. combing your hair
3. going down the slide

Page 97

a. 25°F b. 95°F c. 212°F d. 9°F

Page 98

1. 5¢ 2. 5¢ 3. 10¢

Page 99

Page 100

8 oranges 10 bananas

Page 101

1. Mr. Shivers 3. Ice Bucket
2. Chilly Willy and Snowflake

Page 102

a. hexagon c. square e. rectangle
b. circle d. triangle

Page 103

1. 3 pieces 2. 2 pieces 3. 1 piece 4. 2 pieces

Page 104 *Pictures may vary.*

Page 105

a. 3, 4, 6, 8
b. 17, 19, 20, 21,
c. 49, 50, 53
d. 80, 81, 84, 85
e. 92, 94, 95, 96

Page 106

3 piglets 4 chicks 2 bunnies 5 ducklings

Page 107

4 hot dogs and 1 hamburger
3 hot dogs and 2 hamburgers
2 hot dogs and 3 hamburgers
1 hot dog and 4 hamburgers

Page 108

1. 150 2. 25

Page 109

1. 12 2. 4 3. 4 4. 2

Page 110 100 logs

Page 111

1. Woody Woodchopper
2. Petula Pig Pigs-out
3. Dudley Duck Dives In

Page 112

1. The baby weighs 7 lbs.
2. The adult elephant weighs 1 ton.
3. The dinosaur weighs 900 kg.

Page 113

Farrell—October 31   Farley—November 3
Farrah—October 29   Fario—November 1

Page 114

a. sphere   c. cone
b. cube   d. cylinder

Page 115

a. 34 and 98   c. 3457 and 9875
b. 345 and 987

Page 116

1. Maya   2. 1 quart

Page 117

1. 52 pies   2. 4 pies

Page 118

Page 119

a. 16 oz., 22 oz., 36 oz., 45 oz., 60 oz.
b. 3 oz., 9 oz., 12 oz., 21 oz., 30 oz.

Page 120

The first one is 86 ft.
The second one is 84 ft.

Page 121

1. $2 + 9 = 11$ 3. $9 + 8 = 17$ 5. $18 - 9 = 9$
2. $7 + 8 = 15$ 4. $15 - 6 = 9$ 6. $14 - 8 = 6$

Page 122   96 knights

Page 123

a. 635   b. 487   c. 385   d. 105

Page 124

a. $7 + 7 = 14$ c. $16 - 8 = 8$
b. $7 + 2 = 9$ d. $8 - 2 = 6$

Page 125   56 legs

Page 126

a. four   d. nine   g. six   i. seven
b. three   e. two   h. ten   j. five
c. one   f. eight

Page 127

7 triangles   18 rectangles   29 squares

Page 128

	0	2	4	6	8	10
Monday						
Tuesday						
Wednesday						
Thursday						
Friday						

Page 129

a. 1,119   b. 210   c. 8,280   d. 690

Page 130

35 Banana Bits   40 Blueberry Bites
45 Strawberry Strips

Page 131

1. 96 marshmallows   2. 29

Page 132   51 feet

Page 133   2:40 P.M.

Page 134

1. 12 eggs   2. 24 dozen

Page 135   52 inches

Page 136   48, 54, 852, 536, 552

Page 137

5:45   1:30

8:10   6:25

Page 138   23 bananas

Page 139   6 combinations

yellow	pink	lavender
3	1	1
1	3	1
1	1	3
2	1	2
2	2	1
1	2	2

Page 140   7 times

Page 141   12 windows

Page 142

second pile—12
third pile—17

Page 143   30 drumsticks

Page 144   18 bones

Page 145

Kirby—June   Katy—March

Page 146

Page 147   12:15 A.M.

Page 148

Page 149   Patty, Priscilla, Paul, Petula

Page 150

Porky—68¢   Peter—86¢
Patty—75¢   **Peter has the most!**

Page 151 $1.39

Page 152

Second—10:45
Third—11:30

Page 153   168 feet

Page 154   111 fish

Page 155

Mama Bear—a bowl of cereal
Baby Bear—toast and orange juice
Papa Bear—bacon and eggs

Page 156   45 peanuts for 50¢

Page 157   10:30 A.M.